I0569335

Freedom

Step by Step

A Declaration for Walking in Freedom

Vivian Hart

FREEDOM STEP BY STEP: A Declaration for Walking in Freedom.

Copyright © 2025 All rights reserved—Vivian Hart

No part of this book may be reproduced or transmitted in any form or by any means, graphic, electronic, or mechanical, including photocopying, recording, taping, or by an information storage retrieval system without the written permission of the publisher. The contents and cover of this book may not be reproduced in whole or in part in any form without the express written permission of the author.

Please direct all copyright inquiries to:
daughtersariseministry.8@gmail.com

Paperback ISBN: 978-1-955605-93-9

Cover and Interior Design: B.O.Y. Enterprises, Inc.

Printed in the United States.

Scripture quotations marked (NKJV) are taken from the New King James Version®. Copyright © 1982 by Thomas Nelson. Used by permission. All rights reserved.

Scripture quotations marked (NIV) are taken from The Holy Bible, New International Version®, NIV®. Copyright © 1973, 1978, 1984, 2011 by Biblica, Inc. Used with permission of Zondervan. All rights reserved worldwide. www.zondervan.com

Scripture quotations marked (KJV) are taken from the King James Bible, a work of public domain.

Scripture quotations marked (NLT) are taken from the Holy Bible, New Living Translation, copyright ©1996, 2004, 2015 by Tyndale House Foundation. Used by permission of Tyndale House Publishers, Carol Stream, Illinois 60188. All rights reserved.

"Scripture quotations marked (ESV) are from the ESV® Bible (The Holy Bible, English Standard Version®), © 2001 by Crossway, a publishing ministry of Good News Publishers. ESV Text Edition: 2025. The ESV text may not be quoted in any publication made available to the public by a Creative Commons license. The ESV may not be translated in whole or in part into any other language. Used by permission. All rights reserved."

Scripture quotations marked (GNT) are from the Good News Translation in Today's English Version- Second Edition Copyright © 1992 by American Bible Society. Used by Permission.

Dedication

This book is dedicated to three missing links of our family.

my father - David Pettus Jr
my sister — Kathy Moore
my brother — Gregory Pettus

CONTENTS

Acknowledgements

First and foremost, I would like to thank God for the revelation to write this book. Had it not been for God, I would not be in a place where I am free to share my testimony. When I think about where I was in my life a few years ago, and where I am today, I can truly say that I am in this place because of our Heavenly Father. This journey has not been easy, and I cannot say that if I had a choice, I would not have changed some things. But I can honestly say, that through all that I have been through, God was with me even when I did not realize it at times in my life.

Second, I would like to thank my family: Dennis my husband, Anthony, our eldest son, Adrian our youngest son, Germanie our daughter and Doris our daughter-in-law for supporting my call, my ministry, and my overseas mission work. Thank you for your prayers and encouragement. To my wonderful grandchildren, Aniya, Amaria, Avry, Sophie, Maddilyn and Maddison, thank you for helping to make gloomy, sad days, lively and fun.

To my besties, you all know who you are, thank you for supporting me. There were times when my heart was heavy and the tears were flowing and I would text you all, *"pray for me,"* and you prayed.

I have to say thank you to the great members at Clover A.M.E. Zion Church, my first pastoral charge. This is where God gave me the vision for this book after our Breaking Free Women's Conference. I thank God for sending me to be your under-shepherd. I love you all and I know you love me. Thank you to my four wonderful pastors, Rev. Dr. Charles Darden Jr, Rev. Dr. Carlton Brown, Rev. Ina Culp Harris and Rev. Thelma Gordon and my mother in ministry, Prophetess Carolyn Carr-Simpson for encouraging me and helping to mold me.

Last but definitely not least, the two people who gave me life, my mother Annie Lee, and my father David (deceased) Pettus. Thank you for bringing us up in church. It was because of the both of you that I learned who God is. Thank you for nurturing us and thank you for loving us.

If there is anyone that I forgot, please do not hold it against me, as the saying goes, charge it to my head and not to my heart.

Endorsements

Freedom: A Call to Women, is more than a book, it's a spiritual journey that touches the heart of every woman who has ever carried hidden pain behind a smile. Vivian writes with authenticity, vulnerability, and the anointing of someone who has walked through the fire and come out refined by God's grace.

As I read her story, I could hear the voice of God echoing through every page, calling women to release the bondage of the past and walk boldly in the freedom Christ has already given us. Her transparency and obedience to God's instructions make this not just a testimony, but a movement of healing and deliverance for women everywhere.

This book is a reminder that true freedom begins when we admit our wounds, seek God's presence, and allow Him to transform our pain into purpose. Vivian's obedience to the call of "Freedom" will inspire every reader to seek their own breakthrough and embrace the wholeness that only comes from Christ Jesus.

I highly recommend this powerful work to every woman, pastor, leader, mother, wife, or sister who is ready to live free indeed.

– Rev. Dr. Angela R. Williams
Pastor, Author, and Advocate for Women's Empowerment

Freedom, A Call to Women by Rev. Vivian Hart and based on Galatians 5:1, *"Christ has set us free! Stand, then, as free people, and do not allow yourselves to become slaves again"*(GNT) is a book full of wisdom and knowledge based on having a close and personal relationship with Jesus Christ. Rev. Hart's story takes you on an up close and personal journey of her walk with Christ to learn about grieving and forgiveness that leads to healing and restoration that only comes from God. This is a biblical based book about a personal and spiritual journey that she experienced throughout her life and that we all can learn from. My prayer is that everyone who reads this book is blessed and will hold on to the truths and lessons she shared. Enjoy the journey!

Willie Ruth Johnson, 1st Lady, International Missionary, Restoring Your Heart Facilitator, and life friend in Christ.

Introduction: A Call to Women

Galatians 5:1, *"Christ has set us free! Stand, then, as free people, and do not allow yourselves to become slaves again." (GNT)*

One morning in January 2020, as I was dressing and preparing to leave for my physical therapy appointment, I heard the voice of God say, "Freedom." I paused for a few seconds and said, Lord, what are you telling me? I heard again, "Freedom." But the Lord did not say anything else. I then said, "Ok, Lord." I knew the Lord would tell me more, at a later time. That is how God operates with me, He never gives me all the information at one time. In a rush to finish getting ready for my physical therapy appointment, I grab my red Mary Kay lipstick tube and wrote the word on my bathroom mirror, "Freedom 2020," so that I would not forget. Still not totally understanding what God was saying. I went about my business as usual.

A few days later, I heard God say, "too many women are living in bondage, and it is time for them to walk in freedom." As I pondered on what God said, I knew this to be true because even as a Christian, I was not totally walking in freedom myself. There are many other women just like me, who are not only living in bondage but living behind a mask as though all is well. If you asked them, how are they doing, they are quick to say, "I am blessed and highly favored or too blessed to be stressed."

Many women, including Christian women, are living as though everything is all right, but as my daddy use to say, *"that's a lie and the truth aint in you."* It is a lie because most of us have been taught from childhood how to put on a façade. I am speaking from experience when I say this, simply because women tend to hold on to a lot of past hurts, pain, abuse, unforgiveness and they are living with open wounds. They are blessed but they also have open wounds from the past and the present.

> *"Façade, a false appearance that makes someone or something seem more pleasant or better than they really are."*

Many women experienced pain and hurt in their childhood and they have taken that same hurt and pain from their childhood into their adulthood and they never learned how to acknowledge the pain, process the pain, grieve the pain, and be delivered and healed from their hurt and pain.

What I have discovered from my own experiences and listening to many other women is, unresolved pain does not simply fade away; instead, it becomes a part of our daily lives, influencing how we think, feel, and interact with others. Without learning how to acknowledge the pain, process our emotions, grieve our losses, and seek true healing, we remain bound by the hurts of our past. The inability to work through these difficult experiences leaves us vulnerable to ongoing emotional struggles, hindering our ability to live in freedom and wholeness.

Am I speaking to someone? As you transition from childhood through adolescence and into adulthood, the reality for many is that pain continues to accumulate. Each stage of life can bring new wounds, disappointments, and heartaches, which often pile on top of earlier hurts that were never fully addressed or healed. Rather than fading away, these unprocessed experiences create layers of pain, making it increasingly difficult to break free. This ongoing cycle of unresolved hurt can weigh heavily on your spirit, affecting your sense of self and your ability to move forward in true freedom.

Then for many women with open wounds and unresolve pain, if you married someone who is broken on the inside, who has wounds that have never been healed, that person cannot help you, but often times cause you more pain. Two broke people do not make a whole person.

Many women have been hurt, abused, mistreated, and disrespected because of someone else's brokenness. Women have experienced pain and hurt in their marriages, but they stay, which again causes more built-up pain and hurt. And so, these things have become a bondage for many women. We live in bondage, we work in bondage, we care for our families in bondage, and we serve and worship God to the best of our ability in bondage. Know this also, many preachers and pastors are preaching from the pulpit Sunday after Sunday in bondage. I know this book is addressing mainly women, but the truth of the matter is, pain does not discriminate.

There are many men and women preachers, who are preaching from the pulpit, but many are preaching from a place of bondage, they have been hurt, they are in pain, they have been cut in their hearts and sometimes they are bleeding all over the sheep and do not realize it. Not only are they preaching from a place of brokenness, but they are also ministering from a place of bondage. Preachers get calls all times of the day and night from people who need to be ministered and counseled, and I thank God that He gives us the wisdom and words to be able to give hope to those who are in need. But sometimes when ministers have been cut in their hearts, and their emotions are all over the place, and they are feeling all alone. They need someone to pray for them and minister to them also. As a minister myself, I can relate to Moses in Exodus 17:4, when He cried out to God, I do not know what to do. Moses was facing a bad situation, and he needed God to intervene. Before Moses asks God for help, he first acknowledges he has a problem.

Many people call on family, friends, call the pastor, or talk to coworkers about what they are dealing with, seeking advise on how to handle their problems before they take it to God. Some people shut down and keep everything inside. Is there anyone reading this GUILTY? I was. In the past my coping mechanism to dealing with problems was to shut down. If people, mainly my spouse, would say something to hurt me or make me angry, I SHUT DOWN! Even now, I still sometimes struggle with not going to that place of shutting down. But what I have learned now, when I do shut down, it is to allow God to minister to me and to help me control my temper, so that I can get back to that place of doing what God has anointed me to do. I am striving to become like Moses in taking everything to God first, then God will give you trusted, Spirit-filled people you can talk to if needed.

As Moses asked God, what should I do? I asked God the same question about the women's conference, God what shall I do? I understood that I am limited in my thinking. I understood that I am limited in my knowledge. I wanted this conference to be God's way and His way only. God said this is the year for Freedom, and so, me with my finite mind, said, Lord people have been saying, *"this is the year for freedom,"* for years. There have been hundreds of conferences and seminars for years and women are still in bondage. So, what is the difference with what you are telling me to do than what people have done before? What is it Lord that you are saying to me about this freedom experience?

I am asking God all these questions because I do not have clarity of what He wants me to do. I do not know about you all but growing up I would hear older people say, do not question God. I never heard the reasons why we should not question God, and so as a child I was obedient to the adults. As I became an adult and began to study God's Word, I discovered there were several people in the Bible that questioned God. So, I began to study why these people questioned God and what was the punishment or the outcome. One example is found in Psalm 10:1-18 (ESV) where David says, *"Why, O Lord, do you stand far away? Why do you hide yourself in times of trouble?"* David questioned God because he was in great distress and could not feel the presence of God. So, he cried out, why do you stand far away; God I'm going through some hard times; some dark days and God I feel like You're nowhere around and I need help, where are you God? David questions God because he is hurting and feeling all alone. I think many of us can relate to David's emotional distress and feeling all alone, even feeling at times that God is nowhere near.

Another great example of someone from the Bible who questioned God is found in the Book of Habakkuk 1 verse, we see Habakkuk asking God these questions, *"How long, O Lord, must I call for help? But you do not listen! "Violence is everywhere!" I cry, but you do not come to save" (NLT).* The Prophet Habakkuk is in distress just as David was. He is questioning God. How long must I call for help and you are not coming to save us? I truly can relate to both men; there have been times in my life that I have been in such a dark place that I felt as if no one cared not even God. It was in this dark place, I experienced depression, anxiety, loss of weight; loss of hair and a loss of faith. There were times when I felt like I was going to lose my mind; there were times when I did not want to live anymore because the pain was too much to bear.

I was in bondage to my situations, and I stayed in that place of bondage because I did not know how to get free. I would cry out to God, I would ask God why does it seem like I am always going through stuff. And so, what I found out, God is ok with us asking questions. He can handle our questions. God may not respond when we want Him to but know this, He hears you. If you continue to read the story of David and Habakkuk, you will see that God intervened on both of their behalf. God does not leave His children in a state of brokenness or in bondage, but there is a part that we must participate in our walk towards healing and deliverance.

So, I asked God, why have another Freedom Women's Conference? What is going to be different with this conference than other conferences? God with His infinite being said this to me, yes there have been many conferences encouraging women to walk in freedom, some of those conferences were successful in helping women, but there were some conferences that just stirred the emotions of the people but there was no change on the inside.

Some people have a good idea to have a woman's conference, but here is the difference Many of them were not a God idea. Some gatherings are annual women conferences. I am not saying that is wrong, but it may not be what God is saying to do in that season. We must hear from God. Understanding this, people, even church folk, can come up with a good idea that will move the people's emotions. Because people are hurting and looking for help, they will run from conference to conference without praying and asking God which one to attend. And so, people will experience a high for a moment but then comes the fall.

There is a popular thrill ride a Carowinds Amusement Park in Fort Mill SC, call the Drop Zone Tower. This tower stands 227 feet straight up in the air; it holds numerous people at one time. As this tower is lifting the people up these 227 feet tower slowly, people are feeling the excitement; they are experiencing the thrills; in the moment most of the people are smiling and laughing because they are excited to be going up. Are you seeing this in the spirit?

For years I have heard this phrase, "What goes up must come down." As this tower drops the people at a rate of 56 mph, the laughter then turns into screams; the joy turns into fear; the dry eyes begin to release tears. This is what some conferences do for people. Most people including Christians, we enjoy the highs of a conference, but it is the fall that we do not like after the conference is over, and we do not know how to handle it when the enemy comes up against us. Any time there is an overwhelming of emotions being released, women being set free, delivered and opening up about their struggles, the devil is soon to show up. His job is to kill, steal and destroy and he wants us to stay in bondage.

So, after much prayer and as I listened to God's instructions about this conference, He gave me the names of every person who was to minister, through leading the ladies in worship, to praise dancing before the Lord, to reading the scripture, to welcoming the ladies, to sharing their testimony and ministering to the ladies who would come in bondage.

The difference with this conference was, this conference was a God idea, God ordained, and God led, I was only an obedient vessel. As I pondered on what God was saying about women being in bondage, I thought, Lord, this includes me also. In so many ways I am still in bondage. Is there anyone saying, me too? He reminded me, daughter, this is for you too. And as I said yes, God gave me more pieces for this conference. The conference is ready; the programs are ready, everyone that God said was to participate said yes; I had two prayer conference calls with the participants, which was an awesome move of God;

every participant was excited about the great move of God that was going to take place; the ladies bags had been put together, we were excited and believing God for healing. Then weeks before the conference came Covid-19 and the mandate for restricting the amount of people allowed in a gathering. I must be honest; this did cause me a level of stress and uncertainties. I knew this conference was God ordained but I did not know how it would play out now that a restriction had been put in place. The restriction at the time was no more than fifty people in one gathering and there should be a six-foot distance between each person. I wanted to obey authority, but I also must obey God, and I know that God is not a God of confusion. He is not a God that tells us to do one thing, and He does another. So, again, I go to God in prayer with my concerns.

I had several concerns about the number of people in a gathering. First, because there had been over fifty people who had pre-registered for the conference, and I did not know who would show up. Secondly, my heart told me, if we were at the fifty people count and someone showed up, I did not want to turn them away, because the conference was dealing with women breaking chains: breaking strongholds and walking in freedom. All though women look one way on the outside, we truly do not know what they are dealing with on the inside, or who is on the verge of giving up and ending it all.

So, I go to God with a heavy heart and said, I do not know what to do, you have to work this out. I heard the voice of God say, go to the church for seven days, 30 minutes each day to worship me. I shared my concerns with the church members and told them what God had instructed me to do. I invited the ladies to come but I let them know this was not going to be a time for talking and socializing but to worship. For seven days, I drove to the church which is about a 20-minute drive from my home to worship God for 30 minutes each day for seven days. The first day, the Spirit of God fell so heavily in the church and upon me that I was there over an hour and could barely get up from the floor. I went back the second day, then the third day until my seven days of worship was completed. For those who are familiar with numerology, in the scriptures, seven often symbolizes completion or perfection.

The Hebrew word for seven (*sheba*) both derives from the Hebrew word meaning satisfaction or fullness (*saba*). Genesis tells us that God created the heavens and the earth in six days, and, upon completion, God rested on the seventh day (Genesis 2:1-3 (NIV), *"Thus the heavens and the earth were completed in all their vast array. 2 By the seventh day God had finished the work he had been doing; so, on the seventh day he rested from all his work. 3 Then God blessed the seventh day and made it holy, because on it he rested from all the work of creating that he had done."*

In the context of healing, the prophet Elisha referenced the number seven when he directed Naaman the leper to bathe in the Jordan River seven times to be healed (2 Kings 5:9-14 (NIV), *" So Naaman went with his horses and chariots and stopped at the door of Elisha's house. Elisha sent a messenger to say to him, "Go, wash yourself seven times in the Jordan, and your flesh will be restored and you will be cleansed." But Naaman went away angry and said, "I thought that he would surely come out to me and stand and call on the name of the Lord his God, wave his hand over the spot and cure me of my leprosy. Are not Abana and Pharpar, the rivers of Damascus, better than all the waters of Israel? Couldn't I wash in them and be cleansed?" So, he turned and went off in a rage. Naaman's servants went to him and said, "My father, if the prophet had told you to do some great thing, would you not have done it? How much more, then, when he tells you, 'Wash and be cleansed'!" So, he went down and dipped himself in the Jordan seven times, as the man of God had told him, and his flesh was restored and became clean like that of a young boy").*

Sometimes God will have us to do things that do not make sense to us, to bring about healing and restoration.

It was on the cross that Jesus spoke seven statements in agony at the completion of His earthly duties. The last saying being, *"Father, into Thy hands I commend My spirit,"* Luke 23:46 (KJV).

After my seven days of worshipping and praying, I ask God to allow only the women who need to be there to show up. It is not that other women do not need to walk in freedom, because there are many who do. But what we must understand is, it is more than just showing up to a conference that initiates deliverance. The beginning of deliverance does not start when you show up, but it begins with acknowledging that you are in bondage, and you have a deep desire to be free. You may not understand the totality of your bondage or even when your bondage began, but if you never admit that you are living in bondage, you will never walk in freedom.

What I learned during those seven days of worship and praying is most of the time we try to handle problems that God never intended for us to handle. And when we do that, we cause more stress on ourselves and others who are in our path. Stop trying to handle every problem that comes your way. This is what God told King Jehoshaphat. When the king and the people of Judah and Jerusalem received word that a vast combined army were plotting to attack them, they begin to stress. God told the people to stop stressing, I've got this. The Lord said in 2 Chronicles 20:15 (NLT), *"Listen, all you people of Judah and Jerusalem! Listen, King Jehoshaphat! This is what the Lord says: Do not be afraid! Don't be discouraged by this mighty army, for the battle is not yours, but God's.* If you go back up to 2 Chronicles 20 and read verse 3 and 4, Jehoshaphat was terrified by this news and the vast army. But he did not allow his situation to keep him and the people in a state of fear, the Bible says that he sought the Lord for guidance and then he *"ordered everyone in Judah to begin fasting. So, people from all the towns of Judah came to Jerusalem to seek the Lord's help."*

We have a part to play in our freedom walk. Part of our role is to seek the Lord for help. We cannot just sit around doing nothing expecting God to do it all. Yes, He can handle any problem without our help because He is omnipotent, meaning that God is all powerful. God can do whatever He wants and pleases. God's power is infinite, meaning His power is limitless! But He expects us to do some things. Once I did as King Jehoshaphat did, I sought the Lord in prayer for guidance for the situation at hand, and when I sought God for guidance, He gave me peace. So much peace the morning of the conference, I overslept.

I knew this conference was a God idea; I knew this conference was God ordained, but what I did not know is how God was going to bring it to pass. I had to let go and let God. So often we will not let go and the Lord said that a lot of our bondages are because we keep holding on to that which is holding on to us. Somebody needs to catch that. Anger, we hold on to it. Fear, we hold on to it. Past hurts, we hold on to them. Abandonment, we hold on to it. Abuse, we hold on to it. God has been trying to deliver us but often, we will not let go.

The morning of the conference, after I woke up and realized I had overslept, I rushed to get ready and headed to the church. As I drove to the church with peace, I said, Lord if we have over fifty people, we will find somewhere to put them, even if they have to sit in the fellowship hall with the doors open. Did anyone see how I picked up the stress again? God had already given me peace. He had already told me that it is already worked out. Let me tell you how God operates and how He showed me that He is in control of this conference. We had over seventy-five people to pre-register and purchase tee shirts, but only right at fifty showed up. "Won't He do it!" I honestly believe that everyone who God ordained to be there was there.

I shared earlier that God ordained who was to minister to the ladies. In my obedience in contacting these women, they said yes, (not that I am always obedient, I am still a work in progress). I had no idea that God was going to minister to each of these ladies as they ministered to us. Some of them were dealing with their own bondage issues and pain, yet they felt free enough to share their story at the conference. As a matter of fact, some of the participants wanted to say no when I called them to serve, but God impressed upon their hearts to say yes. God knows what we need before we even ask. I remember a few years ago that God told me, I was to minister to female inmate at Moss Justice Prison in York SC. I told God that I could not do that, because those ladies had too many issues, and I had too many issues myself to help somebody else. God told me, in the process of me helping them, that He would help me. I did not understand how, but I said yes Lord. God allowed me to minister to the female inmates for 5 years. That season in my life was truly a blessing for me. God has many ways of helping His children. How God does things may not make sense to us. God's word tells us in Isaiah 55:8 (NLT), *"My thoughts are nothing like your thoughts," says the LORD. "And my ways are far beyond anything you could imagine."*

The people that showed up for the conference are the ones that God knew needed to be there. He also knew that if certain people were there, some of the women would not be open and honest about their wounds. God knew that some of the women would have come with judgmental spirits, not coming for deliverance but coming to be a spectator. So, God put the fear of the virus and being in a crowd of people in their mind causing them to stay away.

Please do not misunderstand me, I am not saying that all the ladies that did not come are spectators, I am not saying that at all. I personally know some of the women who did not come, and they are true Women of God. There were many that did not come because they had a legitimate concern about the virus because of the unknown and their health challenges. I too had great concerns about the virus and the safety of the women who came.

But we know even before the Covid-19 virus, we have spectators in our churches that come Sunday after Sunday, not necessarily coming to worship, not coming to hear from God, not even coming to fellowship with other believers but coming to hear what somebody is going to share or who's going to cry at the altar, or coming out of tradition. Many come every Sunday not expecting anything from God, not even acknowledging who He is or His power. The apostle Paul describes the nature of people in the last days. He characterized them *as "having a form of godliness but denying its power."* Paul even warns us associating ourselves with them, he says, *"Have nothing to do with such people"* (Timothy 3:5, NIV). But because most of them are our family members, we still tolerate them.

The morning of the conference, I witnessed God do great and marvelous works. Women were free to weep, they were free to share their stories, they were free to acknowledge they were in bondage, they were free to say, they were hurting and they needed help. God knew who needed to be there and He was ready to help set them completely free. I was in awe of what God did at this conference, and how women were able to walk out in freedom.

Jesus has already come and set us free, not partially but completely and wonderfully free! Free from the bonds of sin, free from hurts and pain, free from mental and emotional bondage and free from unforgiveness. God's desire is that his children live a life of freedom, I am not saying without any problems or troubles but free from the traps of Satan. But what I have discovered is, although Christ came to set us free, the enemy have deceived many people in thinking, there is no hope and there is no way out. So, many people stay in bondage from past hurts and pain and unforgiveness. We look whole to the physical eyes, but there are many people who are perpetrating. They are hiding behind a mask because they do not want people to see that they are broken on the inside and living in a state of bondage. So, we go through life as though everything is ok. I know this to be true, because I have ministered to a lot of women who were living a life behind a mask. I myself put on a façade for years, I dressed up my outer appearance so that I could conceal a less pleasant reality. That reality was, I was broken. I lived in a state of brokenness for years. No one told me that there is help for my pain, no one told me that God could put me back together again. As a matter of fact, most people did not even see my pain because I hid it. As I aged, I understand now why some people cannot see your pain because they are drowning in their own pain and sorrow and they are living in their own bondage. So, God said, this is the season that many women will walk in their freedom. The Bible says, *"So if the Son sets you free, you are truly free"* *(NLT).*

Vivian Hart

CHAPTER 1

How Did I End Up Here?

I remember some years ago my daughter had a doctor's appointment in Fort Mill SC. We got into the car, drove down highway 161, merged onto highway 77 north on our way to Fort Mill for the appointment. A lot of times I do not have the radio on when I am driving because it gives me an opportunity to enjoy the quietness or time to think and meditate on God's word and sometimes on my problems. As we were driving on highway 77 north in the quietness, without realizing it, I passed both exits that would have taken us into Fort Mill. That day my mind was so consumed with problems and things that I was dealing with, I missed my exit. When I realized it, I was merging onto highway 485 towards Pineville NC, into a different city from where my daughter's appointment was. As I was merging onto highway 485, I said to myself, how did I end up here? That was just one of many times throughout my life that I have asked myself that question, how did I end up here?

What I have discovered in my later adult years is, sometimes in order to understand how you ended up in a certain place in your life, you have to look back into your past. What I mean by that is many women's childhoods were not perfect. As a matter of fact, it was far from perfect. Many women's childhood involved neglect, emotional, physical, and sexual abuse, rape, abandonment, bullying, and traumatic events. Because there are no perfect people, there are no perfect families. I believe that each family has experienced some type of traumatic event that may still affect some adults today. So, if you want to know the "why's" in your life, take a look at your childhood and be honest about the trauma you went through.

Kaiser Permanente and the Centers for Disease Control and Prevention's 1998 study on adverse childhood experiences determined that traumatic experiences during childhood are a root cause of many social, emotional, and cognitive impairments that lead to increased risk of unhealthy self-destructive behaviors, risk of violence or re-victimization, chronic health conditions, low life potential and premature mortality.

The study identified ten of the most traumatic events or experiences a child is likely to encounter. The consequences of these events can be devastating, and, without effective therapy, these traumatic events can negatively impact the individual for a lifetime.

1. Growing up with a parent/guardian who is an addict or who is a chronic abuser of drugs or alcohol.
2. Growing up in a home where the parent or main caregiver goes to prison.
3. Growing up in a home where the parent has been diagnosed with a mental illness such as schizophrenia or depression.

4. Witnessing their mother being physically abused by their father or her partner.
5. Experiencing emotional abuse -this can range from parents being emotionally unavailable due to long working hours or their own self-absorption, to parents routinely demeaning, scarring, or verbally abusing the child.
6. Experiencing sexual abuse from parents, family members, other children, or anyone in a position of authority or power over the child.
7. Experiencing physical abuse -either in the home by parents who use physical abuse to discipline the child, or outside the home by other authority figures.
8. Losing their primary care giver or parent due to death, divorce, or abandonment.
9. Living with emotional neglect in some ways emotional neglect is the opposite of abuse or mistreatment; it is a failure to act, an omission. Parents fail to notice or respond enough or appropriately to a child's feelings. There is little or no emotional support or validation.
10. Growing up with physical neglect this applies when children are not adequately fed or clothed, kept clean, or kept warm in cold weather.

As the number of experiences increases, the risk of problems from childhood through adulthood also rises. Most everyone that is reading this book would probably fit into one or more of these ten traumatic events. Unfortunately, most children do not receive any type of therapy to help them process what they have experienced. I had to look back at my childhood to better understand my ways, my actions, and my decisions as an adult.

Back in the late 60's my family and I lived in Washington D.C., this is where my brother and I were born. From what I was told, I was a happy child, very independent and enjoyed playing with my brother. One Sunday afternoon my mother needed to go to the store to purchase bread to make our dad lunch for work on Monday. So, we were walking to the store, my mom, another adult cousin, my brother who was 5 and myself, 4 years old at the time. The adults were walking and talking behind us, while me and my brother ran ahead of them, laughing, playing, and picking yellow daisies, and white dandelions that were growing in the grass along the sidewalk. My brother and I spotted a flower at the same times so we both began to run towards the flower, my brother was bigger and faster than me, so he outran me. As he bent over to pick the flower, part of his body, mainly his head, was over the sidewalk and into the street. A car came by not seeing him and struck my brother in his head, ripping off half of his face. His lifeless body laid on the sidewalk covered with blood as my mother and cousin were screaming hysterically.

This was a traumatic event that left my whole family shattered and heartbroken. In the culture that I grew up in, back in the 60s, 70s and 80s, you did not see many people, especially within the African American community seeking help from a counselor or a therapist for help in mental issues. God was their help. We were taught to take all of our problems and cares to Jesus. I genuinely believe that God is a healer, but I also believe that He gives us people whom He has called and anointed as well to help those who are in need. Because seeking outside help was not a part of our culture, neither my mom nor my dad nor did I get counseling to help us process the pain of losing a son and a brother. Not only was this a great loss, but it was a horrific event that happened in front of us. A lot of the events after my brother's death, I do not remember. Years later, after sharing my story in my Christian Counseling class, one of my instructors said this could be a way that my brain has protected me. Things in our home were never the same again after the death of my brother. My mom always says, after the death of a child, you never get over it, but you learn how to live with it. Most people when they experience a traumatic event in their life, things change forever. My mother and my father were crushed, and I had lost my best friend.

After the passing of my brother, my parents moved us to South Carolina where they are originally from. It was different from what I was used to. In DC, the houses were side by side with very little yard and the streets were paved. There were a lot of cars and buildings. There were traffic lights that told you when to go and when to stop. My mom walked me to school, which was not far from where we lived. The only animals I remember seeing were dogs and they did not run loose. It was normal to hear sirens throughout the day. When we moved down south, it was culturally different and not necessarily in a bad way. The area in which we moved was the country. The house we lived in was on a long dirt road; it was land that my mother's grandfather purchased years prior. The neighboring land belonged to my grandfather's brothers in which their families lived on. These brothers understood the importance of owning land. The houses were not side by side. For the first time in my young life, I saw chickens, pigs, cows and creepy slimy sn..kes, you know what I'm talking about. My sister who was 7 years older than me and already living down south moved in with us. So, I lost a brother, moved to a strange place and a sister, whom I did not really know, moved in to share a bedroom with me.

I met a lot of cousins, some my age and some close to my age. Some who were nice and some who were not so nice. Because of my strong northern accent, I was constantly told, "you talk funny". Truth be told, they did too but I did not tell them. Some people may say well that it was kids being kids, but to a child who had become withdrawn because of the loss of my brother, it caused me to withdraw even more. I did not like talking, because people told me I talked funny, and I believe that is when the enemy put a spirit of shyness in my spirit. Webster dictionary defines shyness as the state of being timid, to be reserved or bashful. Shyness can also be looked at as fear and the Bible says that fear does not come from God. Genesis 3 tells us that *Satan is crafty, and He is roaming and seeking whom He can devour.* The enemy does not wait until we reach a certain age before He sneakily attacks and influences people. The world in which we live is proof of that.

I did not understand it until many years later, but that comment made by my cousins down south, "I talk funny" was a negative affirmation that I stored in my mental file cabinet and unknowingly I became ashamed about how I sounded. Is it not strange how we take those few negative affirmations and hold on to them, and we believe the lies of the enemy verses receiving the many positive ones and basing our self-identity on what God's word say about us.

CHAPTER 2

Suffering in Silence

"Suffering is a complex human experience that involves distress, pain, or hardship. It can be physical, mental, or emotional, often linked to circumstances beyond our control."

"Silent, is making no utterance: not speaking or making noise"

After my family moved down south and I became a preteen, the death of my brother did not have a lasting effect on me as much as it did on my mother and father, so I thought. I remember one hot summer day, I laid down to take a nap, when suddenly, I was awakened by a strong sense of paralyzing fear. I could not move; my heart was pounding against my chest. I had tears rolling down my cheeks. I could not speak, and I had a strong fear that someone in my family was going to die. This feeling lasted for several minutes then it passed. I had never experienced this before. I had no idea what had happened to me, and I could not explain it, so I did not tell anyone. I had no idea that what happened to me was only the first of many years of experiencing the same thing except they got worse. Because I was an introvert growing up and I did not know how to communicate my feelings. I suffered many years with these debilitating attacks in silence.

When I was in my twenties, I was watching an infomercial of a lady describing everything that I had been experiencing for years from the paralyzing fear to the heart pounding and the strong sense of fear. This shocked me, that this lady was on tv telling everyone about my secret and I had not spoken with her. But as I continued to listen, she was not talking about me, but she was describing what she was going through. Then she gave it a name, anxiety attacks/panic attacks. I had no idea this thing that had plagued me for years had a name, and I had no idea that this "things" was only going to get worse before it got better.

What are anxiety attacks?

Anxiety attacks are a combination of physical and mental symptoms that are intense and overwhelming. They are more than just regular nervousness. Anxiety at some levels can feel all-consuming. The body kicks into fight-or-flight overdrive, even when there is no tangible danger. For many, it manifests as racing thoughts, chest tightness, dizziness, or an overwhelming sense that something catastrophic is about to happen even when everything is fine on the outside.

People may not realize how much strength it takes to live with and work through these feelings.

According to Forbes Health, "over 40 million adults (19.1% of the population) have an anxiety disorder in the U.S." One survey found that young people are more likely to experience symptoms of anxiety than older adults. In adolescents between 13 and 18 years old, 31.9% are affected by anxiety disorders.

Because of the shame that has been attached to this disorder, many people do not seek help, but they suffer in silence. If you are dealing with this, you are not alone and there is no shame in seeking help, whether it is through therapy, support groups, or other coping tools.

After I found out that I was having anxiety attacks, I still did not tell anyone, I continued to suffer in silence, and I did not seek help. As I got older the anxiety attacks got worse. They had gotten so much worse that I was having multiple attacks in one day. I would have them at home, at work and while I was driving. They would show up anywhere and anytime. As I continued to experience these attacks and other things that I was going through, I began to experience depression. Now, looking back at my life, I can see where the devil really was trying to destroy me and abort my anointing. Many people navigate these overwhelming attacks alone, either because they fear judgment, do not know how to explain what they are feeling, or simply because they believe that no one will understand.

It is unfortunate that many people, men, women, boys, and girls suffer in silence from anxiety attacks. The enemy wants those who suffer from anxiety to suffer in silence, isolated, and disconnected from the believer's community. He thrives in secrecy, where shame, guilt, and fear can grow unchecked. But here's the good news that echoes through scripture: bondage doesn't get the final word, and Satan's holds can be broken, for 2 Timothy 1:7, (NKJV) reminds us, *"For God has not given us a spirit of fear, but of power, love, and a sound mind."* That fear is not from God and He has already equipped you to face it. Isaiah 61:1 says *the Lord came to "bind up the brokenhearted and proclaim freedom for the captives."*

When I look back on my childhood, I remember the constant hum of anxiety that seemed to follow me everywhere I went. I did not understand why this was happening to me. There were days when the fear felt bigger than me, days when I wondered if I would feel normal again and if these attacks would ever go away.' I felt alone because I did not know how to explain what was happening to me. But through it all, I can see now that I was never alone. Even in those anxious moments, God never left my side, even when I could not hear Him over the noise in my head. Even in the moments when my attacks drowned out everything else, God was quietly weaving purpose into my pain. He had a plan for my life, one I could not see then, but one I hold onto now with everything I have.

A beautiful plan designed just for me. Jeremiah 29:11 is one of my favorite scriptures, it reminds me that God has a plan and a purpose for me, *"For I know the plans I have for you,"* declares the Lord, *"plans to prosper you and not to harm you, plans to give you hope and a future" (NIV)."*

If you are reading this book and you have a similar story or a story plagued with pain, I want you to know this: your story is not over either. God has a plan designed especially for you. If there is one thing I have learned on my journey, it is that God can take what was meant to break us and turn it into something beautiful. He can turn anxious hearts into brave ones. I am living proof. My story is not just about the anxiety that tried to hold me back, but about the faith that carried me forward.

CHAPTER 3

"Broken"

"Broken, having been fractured or damaged and no longer in one piece or in working order"

After the tragic death of my brother, our family was broken mentally and emotionally. I cannot imagine the emotional distress my parents endured losing a child. Heartbroken probably does not describe how they were feeling. They were broken from losing a child and I was broken from losing my brother, my best friend and playmate. As I said earlier, in our culture, when tragedy hits, especially in the 60's, our culture seldom sought professional help. We lived our lives the best we could with open wounds and a crushed spirit. Nothing shatters the heart like losing someone you love. People say time heals all wounds, but I have learned that time alone does not heal but God does. Only He can reach into the places where loss lives. Only He can sit with us in the dark nights of grief and whisper that our broken hearts are safe in His hands.

Growing up with brokenness whether it is emotional, relational, or spiritual can shape a person in profound ways. It often means navigating life with wounds that others cannot see and learning to build strength in places where there was once pain. Brokenness doesn't scare God. In fact, it draws Him close. When David was facing a time of fear and vulnerability, he wrote Psalm 34:18, (NIV) *"The Lord is close to the brokenhearted and saves those who are crushed in spirit."* This is one of the most tender promises in Scripture.

It speaks directly to those moments when pain feels unbearable and the soul feels shattered. It is not just poetic; but it is deeply personal. It reminds us that God does not stand far off when we are hurting. He draws near, offering comfort, presence, and peace. He saves those who are crushed in spirit, not just from external trouble, but from the internal weight of sorrow, despair, or brokenness. When your heart is broken, God does not wait for you to put yourself back together. He meets you in your brokenness and sits with you in the silence and gently lifts you toward healing.

I spent years pretending I was fine when I was not. No amount of pretending can fix brokenness, but God can. Anxiety attacked my peace and fear paralyzed my hope. For years I masked my insecurities until I realized help is already here. When Christ went to the cross, He took on every broken thing: our fears, our shame, our wounds, our sins and *by His stripes, we are healed.* Brokenness is not the end of your story but with God, it is only the beginning. In my brokenness, I found His strength. In my weakness, I discovered His grace. And piece by piece, God has made me whole again.

Losing my brother, then my father and my sister have taught me that brokenness is not the end. It is a reminder that this world is not our home. It is where we grieve, but it is also where we find hope. I know that one day every tear will be wiped away. Hope tells us, that the same God who heals anxiety, fear, and shame also holds our grief, tenderly, patiently, until the day we see our loved ones again.

If you are broken today know this: there is nothing so shattered that God cannot heal. Nothing is so lost that He cannot restore. Nothing so broken that God cannot put back together. There is a metaphor used in Jeremiah chapter 18 where God tells the prophet Jeremiah to go to the potter's house and watch the clay being reshaped. Even when marred, the clay is not thrown away, but it is transformed into something beautiful and useful.

Even in the midst of loss and fractured dreams, I have come to realize that God's grace does not merely mend what is shattered, it transforms brokenness into the foundation of something new. Each day brings renewal and restoration from our scattered pieces. He heals our brokenness, and He turns it into something beautiful. During the quiet seasons that followed the loss of my brother, my father, and my sister, I discovered that true healing did not come through my own efforts or attempts to push through the pain. Instead, it unfolded as I surrendered my pain to God.

Healing was not something I could force; it was a gradual journey, marked by moments of letting go and allowing myself to feel the sorrow that weighed so heavily on my heart. With time, I began to realize that within the depths of my sorrow, there was a hidden strength, a quiet courage waiting to be uncovered. Each step forward required me to trust that healing was possible, even when I could not see it. By surrendering to the process and embracing my brokenness, I slowly found the courage to move forward, allowing grace and hope to take root beneath the weight of my grief. There were days when hope felt faint, yet it was enough to usher me into the next day. Each small step was a testimony that restoration is possible with Christ. My heart, once fractured by grief, started to move toward freedom not a forgetting, but a living that honors both the pain and the promise of healing.

In the quiet aftermath of grief, where words often fail and silence settles heavily, I came to understand that healing is neither swift nor simple; but it is shaped by faith, grace and trusting God to heal the broken places. Sometimes, restoration begins with simply allowing ourselves to be where we are broken, longing, questioning, and trusting that God is present in the fragments. Gradually, each day became a testament to strength, as God's light illuminated the dark path, and the assurance of being there in my deepest pain. It is this steadfast nearness, this faithful presence in heartache, which transforms our wounds into hope that carries us forward toward freedom and newness even as we honor all that has been lost.

In the midst of overwhelming loss and the quiet ache that lingered long after, I discovered that healing rarely arrives as a sudden revelation but rather as a gentle unfolding, marked by moments of unexpected comfort and the persistent whisper of hope. Grief taught me to lean into faith, to accept that restoration is a journey shaped not only by pain, but by the assurance that God is intimately present in every shattered fragment of our lives. Each day forward became an act of trust; with every breath, grace began to mend what was fractured, layering wisdom and compassion over sorrow's remnants. It was in this place of brokenness, I learned to see the beauty in my wounds, knowing that even through suffering, God was weaving new purpose and strength.

CHAPTER 4

"Living In Bondage"

Bondage, "the state of being enslaved."

Bondage is a word that makes people uncomfortable, and it should. When we hear the word bondage, we think of chains, shackles, and iron bars. But bondage also refers to a state of being bound or restrained physically, emotionally, or spiritually. Thayer's Greek Lexicon defines the word bondage, as *"to make a slave of"* or metaphorically to "make myself a bondman."

When we think of bondage, we think of people ripped from their homes, stripped of dignity, and forced to live as less than what God intended. Yet bondage is not always visible; sometimes its grip is silent, slipping into corners of our hearts where old wounds linger, and unspoken fears quietly take root. In the hidden parts of our daily life, it can manifest as patterns that we cannot break or as memories we cannot escape, chaining us to moments that no longer serve our becoming. But even in these unseen prisons, the longing for freedom stirs and a gentle but persistent call to step beyond bondage and reclaim the hope of Christ. It is in recognizing these hidden chains, in naming the burdens we quietly carry, that we begin to loosen their hold, opening ourselves to the possibility of transformation. The journey toward deliverance is both inward and upward, requiring faith not only to trust in what is unseen but also to believe that healing can emerge from the depths of our most silent struggles.

What I have come to understand is that bondage does not always look like iron chains or visible bruises. Sometimes, it is invisible. Sometimes, it lives inside of you. Bondage often hides in subtle places, as a lingering guilt, a silent fear, a memory that quietly binds our spirit without anyone else knowing. It may creep into our routines of daily life, weaving itself into our thoughts and habits until we scarcely recognize its weight. Yet, beneath every silent struggle, freedom is waiting. There is a desire to be free but most often we fail to walk of the path of freedom. Or simply we do not know the path to take to freedom, so we remain in bondage, and we remain broken.

In those moments, I learned that true freedom begins with honest acknowledgement: naming what has bound us and daring to believe God for deliverance. The Bible offers a clear message about God's offering His children freedom. God desires to set His people free. Knowing what the Bible says about bondage can help us find freedom and hope. God's word reminds us that we are never alone and that God cares about our struggles. Whether it is physical, emotional, mental, or spiritual bondage, the Bible teaches that true freedom is found in Christ. Galatians 5:1 (KJV), reminds us, *"Stand fast therefore in the liberty by which Christ has made us free, and do not be entangled again with a yoke of bondage."*

When I was young, anxiety was my master. It told me when to sit down, when to be afraid, when to believe I was not good enough. I walked around every day wearing invisible chains that nobody could see but me. But God... He is the chain breaker. These words, Christ has come to set us free, mean everything to me now. Because I know now that true freedom does not come from where you live or what you own, it comes when we allow Christ to set us free. It comes when you realize that you do not belong to fear anymore. You belong to Him. When I look back now even into my adulthood, I see that every chain I carried fear, shame, worry was no match for the power of Jesus Christ. He did not just soothe my anxiety; He broke its grip. He did not just calm my fears; He gave me courage to stand in the light.

Christ sets us free from bondage, all bondage. Not just the things the world can see, but the prisons no one knows we are locked in. He can unlock the doors we think will never open. He turns slaves into sons and daughters. He turns prisoners into praise singers. He turns broken hearts into testimonies.

Mental bondage, spiritual bondage, and emotional bondage truly do relate to slavery because all three will strip you of your identity; steal your joy, and try to convince you, this is all you will ever be (but the devil is a lie). Just as generations fought for freedom from physical slavery, we must stand up and fight for freedom in our minds and spirits. And the good news is we do not fight alone.

The same God who parted the Red Sea, made the lion to become a pillow, was in the fiery furnace with three Hebrew boys and opened prison doors is still showing up, delivering people, and breaking chains today. God sent Jesus *to proclaim freedom for the prisoners and recovery of sight for the blind, to set the oppressed free.*

In our struggles, we often forget the immense power that Christ holds in breaking our chains. When facing the burdens that keep us bound whether visible or invisible it is easy to lose sight of the freedom offered through faith. Yet, the message of hope is clear: Christ's power is not limited by the weight or nature of our struggles. In our own limited human understanding, we often find ourselves putting God in a box and limiting Him, but the Word of God tells us that we serve a God who is unlimited in power. Here are a few scriptures on God's power:

- 1 Chronicles 29:11 (NLT), *"Yours, O LORD, is the greatness, the power, the glory, the victory, and the majesty; for all that is in heaven and in earth is Yours."*

- Job 36:22-24(NLT), *"God's power is unlimited. He needs no teachers to guide or correct him. Others have praised God for what he has done, so join with them."*

- Psalms 29:4(NLT), *"The voice of the Lord is powerful; the voice of the Lord is full of majesty."*

- Psalms 33:8-9(NLT), *"Let all the earth fear the LORD; let all the inhabitants of the world stand in awe of Him! For He spoke, and it came to be; He commanded, and it stood firm."*

- Psalm 147:5(NLT), *"Great is our Lord and abundant in strength; His understanding is infinite."*

- Matthew 8:27. *"The men were amazed and asked, 'What kind of man is this? Even the winds and the waves obey him!'"*

Because God has power to calm the winds and waves, surely, He is able to shatter the bonds of fear, shame, and worry, releasing us from the prisons that confine our hearts, minds body and soul. When we trust Him, Christ loosens the grip of what binds us and brings us closer to true freedom and healing. His love transforms our brokenness into testimony, and His strength turns our bondage into praise. Relying on Christ's power, we find the courage to move forward, knowing that deliverance is not only possible but promised to those who believe.

We might find ourselves feeling trapped and hopeless, it is important to remember that He has already overcome every hardship. When we lean on Him, we can find the strength we need to break free from anything that seeks to bind us. Each scripture reminds us that we do not fight these struggles alone, as Christ is our advocate and our source of strength.

We can trust that the chains we carry, and those silent, persistent burdens no longer hold authority over our lives. In surrendering our struggles, we discover that hope is not just a distant promise, but a living presence that grows stronger within us each time we choose faith over fear and truth over the lies that the enemy has told us. Each decision to trust God, each moment of courage, loosens another link in the invisible chain. We will find ourselves moving from darkness to light, no longer defined by the weight of our bondage but by the freedom that is our birthright, healing is not a sudden event, but it becomes a daily journey. And as we are on the journey of healing, we have assurance that we are never alone, because Jesus walks beside us, and he is leading us toward a future unshackled and full of promise.

I am not saying I never feel anxious anymore, but I am saying anxiety is no longer my master. So, to the anxious child I was and to anyone still feeling those chains gripping hold to your life, I say to you: Freedom is possible; deliverance is possible. Someone reading this book may be thinking, you do not know my story, you do not know what that person did to me. You don't know the pain and hurt I've experienced. That is true, I don't know your story, but God does and there is nothing too hard for God to handle.

The door is open, walk out of your prison; walk out of whatever is keeping you in bondage. Step by step, you can walk into your destiny with the One who came to set captives free.

CHAPTER 5

"What The Devil Meant For Bad..."

devil, (from Greek diabolos, "slanderer" or "accuser"), the spirit or power of evil.

Satan is known by many names according to the word of God. Adversary (opponent), 1Peter 5:8; Accuser of our brethren, Revelation 12:10; Antichrist (opponent of the Messiah), 1John 4:3; Beelzebub, Luke 11:15; Crooked serpent, Isaiah 27:1; Enemy, Matthew 13:39; Father of Lies, John 8:44; Liar, John 8:44; Murderer, John 8:44.

Satan is described in the Bible as a roaring lion, because lions stalk quietly, trying to remain undetected by its prey, so it can strike, kill, and devour. The Bible also describes Satan as a thief and says that Satan comes to kill, steal and destroy, John 10:10 (NIV) reads, *"The thief comes only to steal and kill and destroy."* But Jesus said, *"I have come that they may have life, and have it to the full.* When the Apostle Peter described Satan in these terms, he was writing to believers, meaning they were not at risk of going to hell.

The Apostle Peter described Satan as the adversary in 1 Peter 5:8. In the biblical literature, the term *"adversary"* is used to describe an opponent or enemy. In the Old Testament, the Hebrew word "Satan" is often translated as *"adversary."*

In Job 1:6-7 , we read, *"One day the sons of God came to present themselves before the Lord, and Satan also came with them. 'Where have you come from?' said the Lord to Satan. 'From roaming through the earth,' he replied, 'and walking back and forth in it."* The adversary in Job is depicted as a challenger to Job's righteousness, questioning his motives and seeking to test his faithfulness to God. This portrayal highlights the role of the adversary as one who seeks to undermine the relationship between God and His people.

The adversary, particularly in the form of Satan, is a central figure in Christian theology, representing the embodiment of evil and opposition to God's will. The adversary's role is to tempt, accuse, and deceive, as seen in the temptation of Jesus in the wilderness (Matthew 4:1-11). Jesus' victory over the adversary in this account serves as a model for believers in resisting temptation and remaining faithful to God.

For believers, the presence of an adversary serves as a reminder of the spiritual battle that exists in the world. This recognition calls for vigilance and spiritual discernment, encouraging believers to remain steadfast and intentional in their faith journey. As the enemy seeks to sow confusion and lead astray, it is essential to stay rooted in truth and rely on divine strength, knowing that every trial is an opportunity to draw closer to God and deepen our trust in His promises. With each challenge, believers are invited to fortify ourselves with prayer, wisdom, and the support of a faith community, embracing the assurance that victory is found not in isolation, but through persistent reliance on the One who has already overcome.

We are called to be vigilant, equipped with the armor of God (Ephesians 6:10-18), and to stand firm in our faith.

The Apostle Peter was warning those who already belonged to Christ that the enemy's attacks are relentless, seeking to undermine their faith and distract them from the path God has set before them. The adversary prowls, not to claim their souls, but to sow seeds of doubt, fear, and division, hoping to hinder their walk and disrupt their peace. Yet, knowing his tactics and recognizing his many disguises empowers believers to stand firm, clinging to the promises and armor of God. With this awareness, each challenge becomes an opportunity to trust more deeply, resist more boldly, and move forward with courage, remembering that victory has already been secured through Christ. Therefore, we must *"Be sober-minded; be watchful. Your adversary the devil prowls around like a roaring lion, seeking someone to devour,"* 1 Peter 5:8 (NLT). As we understand the nature of our spiritual enemy, we are reminded that we do not fight alone, and the grace and strength given to us are more than sufficient to overcome every scheme set against us.

In the Old and New Testament, and today's time, people who are followers of God have an enemy and his name is Satan. Until we know who he is and what his purpose and assignment is, we will struggle to win the battle. Understanding who Satan is helps believers recognize the actions, schemes, plots and plans of the enemy, and can help us be alert and vigilant as he is prowling to and from, seeking whom he can devour, destroy, consume, crush, damage, dismantle, end, eradicate, kill, ruin, sabotage, shatter, smash, and wipe out. We have heard the saying, "why do bad things happen to good people. One reason is because Satan is on a mission and there are no age limits, gender, race creed, or color he will not use or attack. Satan has influenced many people to cause harm on people including children.

Although Satan has a mission, God has a plan. For the Bible says, *"what the enemy meant for harm, God can use it for our good."* This scripture is found in the Book of Genesis, the 50th chapter. In this book, we find the story of Joseph and his family. Joseph was Jacob's eleventh son and Rachel's first. Joseph had ten older brothers and one sister and one younger brother. Jacob's children were blessed according to the covenant God had made with Abraham. Although all of Jacob's children were blessed, there was a special love for his son Joseph because he was born in his father's old age, (Genesis 37:3). Jacob had a love so great for Joseph that he gave him a coat of many colors. The coat symbolized not only Jacob's love for Joseph but also favoritism for him over his brothers.

Joseph's brothers hated him because of his dreams and his father's favor (Genesis 37:3-4). Their jealousy led them to strip him of his robe, throw him into a pit, and sell him into slavery. It was betrayal layered with rejection, abandonment, and injustice. Joseph would find himself in physical bondage as well as emotional bondage. Although this was Jospeh's fate, it was not the end of Joseph's journey. Despite being stripped of comfort and cast into unfamiliar territory, Joseph's unwavering trust in God allowed him to navigate betrayal and adversity without losing hope. In the midst of his trials, Joseph's character was refined and his gifts made room for him. Each setback became a steppingstone towards his purpose, affirming that God's presence remained with him even in the darkest valleys and that redemption was unfolding far beyond what he could see.

I am sharing Joseph's story because although we are loved, we are blessed. Maybe we are favored in the eyes of some, and God has a plan and purpose for our lives, we are still not exempt from life's struggles, troubles, and disappointments.

Joseph's journey was encompassed by jealousy, hatred, betrayal, rejection, abandonment, and injustice. It was members of his own family that caused him pain. But his journey was also encompassed by forgiveness, restoration and divine favor, not from his earthly father but from his Heavenly Father.

Although our journey may include all of these things and more that Joseph had to endure, God is still in control of our destiny and our future. God told Jeremiah, *"For I know the plans I have for you,"* declares the Lord, *"plans to prosper you and not to harm you, plans to give you hope and a future."* Jeremiah 29:11 (NIV).

It may not look like the plans God has for you are coming to fruition, but just as Joseph's journey unfolded through adversity and unexpected detours, we can trust that every season, even those marked by pain or uncertainty serves a greater purpose. The setbacks and struggles we face may challenge our faith, yet they are often the very places where God's promises begin to take shape behind the scenes. As we remain steadfast, holding on to hope and walking in obedience, we discover that

God is working all things for our good, weaving restoration, favor, and peace into the very being of our lives. Just as Joseph's story revealed, what was meant to harm us can become the very foundation upon which blessings are built, reminding us that God's plans are always unfolding, even when we cannot see them in the moment.

The enemy meant harm for Joseph, but God used what Joseph went through to bring restoration to his people and to extend grace to those who hurt him. Nothing we go through is wasted. The challenges, wounds, and brokenness we experience can become instruments of healing when surrendered to God. By allowing God to work through our pain, heal our open wounds and to put our brokenness back together, we can become vessels of hope and reconciliation, not only for ourselves but for those around us.

CHAPTER 6

Forgiveness

Forgiveness, a conscious, deliberate decision to release feelings of resentment or vengeance toward a person or group who has harmed you, regardless of whether they actually deserve your forgiveness

Forgiveness is a broad and intense topic and by no means am I speaking from a professional view. I can only speak from my own experiences. Over time, I discovered that forgiveness is not a one-time event but an ongoing process and a choice we must make again and again as wounds resurface or memories return. Though it is often difficult, choosing to release people has allowed me to experience freedom and healing, enabling me to see those who have hurt me with compassion rather than anger. In surrendering my pain to God, I learned that forgiveness was less about the other person and more about the peace and restoration I needed in my own heart. I remember being attacked by a person who I considered family. Truthfully, I was blindsided and never seen the attack coming.

As I reflected on the incident, my initial reaction was to believe it was simply a misunderstanding. However, as I replayed the events in my mind, negative thoughts began to take hold. The enemy whispered doubts, saying things like, "You've only been nice to them and now this is how they treat you." These thoughts fueled my anger and led to feelings of resentment toward those who had attacked me.

Even after my attackers apologized, I found it difficult to move past the attack. Although I made attempts to be cordial, deep down I did not want any further involvement with them. The truth was, my heart was hardened against those who had wronged me, and I struggled to let go of the anger. In that moment, I recognized that Satan had not only used them in the situation, but he had also used me, by allowing bitterness to take root and influence my actions.

Unforgiveness lingered within me for a long period, and I found myself surprisingly content to remain in that state. It was not until I came to the realization that holding onto unforgiveness is contrary to the word of God so, I felt compelled to change. In response, I spoke out loud, declaring, "I forgive them." I genuinely wanted to forgive and believed I had done so, but the reality was different. Each time I encountered those who had falsely accused me, feelings of resentment would resurface, revealing that my forgiveness had not yet taken root.

I recognized that I was still struggling to forgive, so, I turned to God in prayer, pouring out my heart and earnestly asking Him to help me truly forgive my attackers. This was not a one-time request; I found myself returning to God multiple times, seeking His help to release the bitterness and anger. Through this repeated act of surrender, I came to understand an important truth: simply saying that we forgive someone does not guarantee that forgiveness has actually taken place within our hearts. When we hold onto unforgiveness, we keep ourselves in bondage, unable to experience the freedom and peace that comes from genuine forgiveness. I can truly say, after much prayer and submission to God's will, I was able to forgive and walk out of bondage.

I am fully aware that the story I have shared about being attacked and hurt is not compatible to what some of you may have endured. Many of you have experienced wounds and unspeakable pain inflicted upon you, sometimes by those closest to you. For some, the attackers were family members or individuals who were supposed to love and protect you. For others, the pain came from strangers. Regardless of who caused the harm, the reality is that Satan used these people to bring pain into your life, and that pain has remained with you for years.

Perhaps you find yourself in a place similar to where I once was, desiring to forgive your abuser but feeling trapped by the depth of your pain. The bondage of unforgiveness can be so overwhelming and persistent that you do not know how to release yourself from its grip. If this resonates with you, know that you are not alone in your struggle to forgive, and that healing is possible with time, intention, surrendering and with God's help.

When someone hurts you, it is natural to feel anger and resentment. Holding on to these emotions, however, can leave you feeling trapped and in bondage. The alternative is to choose forgiveness, which allows you to move forward and experience true freedom. While this choice can be difficult and may seem easier said than done, it is an essential step toward healing.

At times, letting go of pain and embracing forgiveness is not something we can do on our own. If you find yourself stuck in hurt and unable to move forward, the first step is to acknowledge your situation, admit to yourself that you are struggling and recognize that you need help.

Once you have acknowledged your need, seek God for guidance and support. Turning to Him in times of struggle can provide the strength and direction needed to walk the path of forgiveness and liberation from the pain that holds you captive.

The Bible offers numerous scriptures that affirm God's presence and care in times of pain.

Psalm 34:18 (NIV), *"The Lord is close to the brokenhearted and saves those who are crushed in spirit."*

Isaiah 41:10 (NIV), *"So do not fear, for I am with you; do not be dismayed, for I am your God. I will strengthen you and help you; I will uphold you with my righteous right hand."*

2 Corinthians 12:9 (NIV), *"But he said to me, 'My grace is sufficient for you, for my power is made perfect in weakness.'"*

Psalm 55:22 (NIV), *"Cast your cares on the Lord and he will sustain you; he will never let the righteous be shaken."*

God has also gifted some people to help those who have experienced trauma, abuse, neglect, abandonment, hurt, and those who are stuck because of pain. These individuals offer understanding, guidance, and compassion to those who are struggling with the weight of past wounds. By seeking support from those whom God has equipped to help, you can find encouragement and practical assistance as you move toward forgiveness and healing. Their presence and wisdom can be a vital part of your journey, reminding you that you do not have to walk this path alone and that help is available for those who need it.

There is so much more that can be said and has already been written on the importance and benefits of forgiving. I am closing this chapter with this, according to Mayo Clinic, forgiveness is a personal journey that can take time and effort. It is essential to remember that forgiving someone does not mean you have to maintain a relationship with them or excuse their behavior. Instead, it is about freeing yourself from the emotional burden of anger and resentment, allowing you to move forward with your life. By embracing forgiveness, you can cultivate a sense of peace and emotional well-being.

CHAPTER 7

Finding Your Peace

Peace, to be complete or whole" or "to live well."

Peace plays a vital role in our lives. It creates a sense of security, respect, tolerance, stability, and well-being to pursue goals without threats. When we allow God's peace to fill our hearts, it empowers us to stand firm in the face of adversity and to respond to others with kindness and patience, even when challenged. This divine peace fosters an inner environment where hope flourishes, relationships are restored, and burdens are lifted, enabling us to move forward with clarity and confidence. As we embrace this peace, it not only anchors us during life's storms but also becomes a guiding light that shapes our interactions and choices, reflecting God's presence in all aspects of our journey.

Peace is an essential foundation for our daily lives, nurturing a sense of security and stability that allows us to pursue our goals without fear or distraction. It cultivates an atmosphere of respect and tolerance, even towards those who do not respect us. When we welcome God's peace into our hearts, it gives us the strength to remain steadfast in adversity, empowering us to respond to others with kindness and patience, even in challenging situations.

For many years, my sense of peace was unsettled due to the painful trauma of losing loved ones. This deep loss left me feeling vulnerable and exposed, creating open wounds in my heart that lingered. Alongside this grief, I struggled with not fully understanding my identity in Christ. The uncertainty and confusion surrounding who I was in Him compounded the challenges I faced, preventing me from experiencing true wholeness and healing. These unresolved issues became obstacles to peace, keeping me in a place of emotional unrest and making it difficult to move forward in life. My peace was unsettled and my hope at times was dim.

The challenges I faced weighed heavily on my heart, causing uncertainty and a sense of unrest within. During these times, I struggled to hold onto hope as the storms of life threatened to overshadow the assurance I once felt. The disruption of peace left me feeling vulnerable, questioning how I could move forward and whether restoration was truly possible. Yet, even in these seasons of turmoil, I learned that acknowledging my unsettled peace was the first step toward healing. God's peace would eventually anchor my soul and guide me back to a place of wholeness and confidence.

This divine peace transforms our inner world, fostering hope and restoring broken relationships. It lifts burdens, enabling us to move forward with clarity and confidence. As we embrace this peace, it becomes an anchor during life's storms and a guiding light that shapes our discissions and choices. In doing so, we reflect God's presence throughout all aspects of our journey, allowing His peace to influence every step we take.

Peace does not mean that life will be free of challenges, difficulties, or adversities. Instead, the peace of God equips us to face our challenges with resilience and hope. While difficulties and storms are inevitable in life, God's peace serves as a steadfast anchor for our souls. This peace empowers us to remain resilient and hopeful, even when circumstances threaten to shake our faith. Unlike worldly peace that depends on favorable external conditions, the peace of God flows from a deep trust in His sovereignty and unwavering love. By inviting God into our struggles and surrendering our anxieties, we experience a profound sense of completeness and well-being that transcends human understanding.

In moments of uncertainty, divine peace provides the assurance we need to endure, to forgive, and to move forward with grace. It becomes a source of healing and restoration, not only for us but also for those around us. As we cultivate God's peace in our hearts, we prepare ourselves for new beginnings and the freedom that lies ahead. We can trust that God is working all things together for our good. As we nurture this peace within ourselves, it becomes a source of healing and restoration.

CHAPTER 8

Declaring Your Freedom

"Freedom, the state of not being imprisoned or enslaved."

When we hear the term "imprisonment," our minds often immediately picture someone confined behind bars or a person who has been incarcerated for a crime they committed or perhaps someone who is falsely imprisoned. However, not all prisons are built from steel bars or surrounded by wire fences. Many people live in prisons that have no physical barriers. These are prisons without bars or walls, yet they are just as real and confined as any correctional facility. Emotional prisons, mental prisons, and spiritual prisons can hold individuals back, shaping their lives and experiences in profound ways. Recognizing these invisible prisons is the first step toward acknowledging the struggles that many people face, even when they are not outwardly visible.

The prisons that do not involve physical confinement often have a powerful grip on our lives. These prisons enslave our minds, our hearts, and our emotions. While some people may appear to walk freely, moving about without restrictions, they are secretly bound in their thoughts, feelings, and pain, unable to experience true freedom. Countless individuals are trapped within these invisible prisons. Fear, shame, grief, unforgiveness, addiction, rejection, abandonment, regrets, negative thinking, guilt, and self-doubt are just some of the strongholds that keep people in bondage. These inner struggles are often hidden from the outside world but are deeply felt and can be just as restrictive as any physical barrier. It is important to reflect and ask yourself: What is your invisible prison? What are you in bondage to? What has become your stronghold? Recognizing these areas of captivity is the first step toward seeking healing and freedom.

Perhaps your invisible prison is built from past regrets, lingering unforgiveness, fear of failure, or the pain of rejection that you carry quietly within. Maybe it is a cycle of negative self-talk or unresolved trauma that you experienced as a child or young adult, which is holding you back, causing you to be stuck in anger and pain, making you feel unworthy or unable to move forward. Whatever your stronghold may be, know that you are not alone. Many people silently struggle with unseen chains that hinder their growth and keep them from experiencing true freedom. Yet, there is hope and healing available.

When you acknowledge these hidden prisons and invite God into those secret spaces, you open the door for healing and transformation. He specializes in breaking chains, renewing minds, and restoring hearts, empowering you to walk in the fullness of your identity and purpose. As you begin to confront and surrender these strongholds, remember that your journey toward freedom is not just for yourself, but also serves as a testimony and encouragement to others seeking release from their own invisible bonds. The longer we are imprisoned to the things listed above and others, the longer they become a stronghold over our lives.

Strongholds can manifest as negative thought patterns, unresolved trauma, or sin that keeps individuals from experiencing God's fullness.

We experience enslavement whenever anything other than God takes control over our lives. In many cases, if we are honest with ourselves, these spiritual prisons are often self-imposed. While it is true that some individuals are held captive by the actions or choices of others, the consequences remain significant regardless of the source.

These forms of bondage impact us deeply. They stand in the way of us reaching our fullest potential and prevent us from truly experiencing peace, joy, happiness, and love. Not only do these prisons hinder our ability to receive these blessings, but they also block us from sharing them with others.

A few years ago, the ministers from my home church participated in an outreach ministry at Moss Justice Correctional Facility in York SC. Twice each month, on Sunday mornings before our worship service began, we would visit the prison. Each minister took turns delivering a message, and it was expected that all ministers attend, regardless of whether it was their turn to speak that day.

One Sunday morning, I found myself sitting quietly in the back corner. During that time, I sensed a distinct and unmistakable call from the Lord to enter into prison ministry.

This calling felt different from our routine Sunday morning prison visits; it was clear and direct. Yet, despite the clarity of the call, I was not immediately willing to accept this new assignment. My reluctance stemmed from my own inner struggles. I was deeply aware of living in my own invisible prison and questioned how I could possibly help others when I felt so confined and limited myself.

When the Lord spoke to me that this was the place where I was meant to minister, I found myself saying, "No, Lord, I have too many problems and issues to help someone else." My attention was consumed by my own struggles and by everything I had endured and the challenges I was still facing in that moment. I could not see any value within myself that could benefit others. My thoughts and focus were distorted, and clouded by the enemy, making it difficult for me to believe that I could be of any help to anyone else.

The Lord spoke to me with clarity, assuring me, "As you are helping others, I will help you." This promise became a turning point in my journey. After wrestling with reluctance and uncertainty, I finally surrendered and said yes to God, marking the beginning of my prison ministry.

As I followed God's direction, I named the ministry "Breaking Free Bible Study and Counseling." For five years, I faithfully visited Moss Justice Correctional Prison twice a month, ministering to the female inmates. This commitment became a significant part of my spiritual walk and personal growth. What I know now, God was preparing me to minister to women with invisible bars.

At the beginning of this ministry, I encountered a crucial challenge: the women were hesitant and reluctant to open up to me. Unsure of how to develop trust and connection, I turned to prayer, seeking guidance from the Lord on how to make the inmates feel comfortable with me. God responded with clear instructions, He said, if I wanted the ladies to open up and share their stories, I needed to take the first step by sharing my own. This instruction was difficult for me to accept and practice, as I was naturally an introvert and accustomed to keeping my problems and struggles private. I found it hard to express my feelings and, truthfully, did not feel as though there was anyone with whom I could truly be vulnerable with.

There were times when the weight on my heart felt overwhelming, and I needed to open up and talk. What I found time after time, when I would reach out to close friends for help, I often found myself in the role of the listener, absorbing their struggles instead of having an opportunity to express myself. Instead of finding the freedom to release my tears and share my pain, I would set aside my needs and continue, suppressing what I was feeling inside. This became a recurring pattern in my life that persisted for many years. Through these experiences, I have come to understand the profound importance of truly listening to others. To anyone reading this, I want to encourage you to intentionally practice the art of listening. Sometimes, simply being there to listen can make an incredible difference and it may even be a matter of life and death for someone who needs to be heard.

My prison ministry turned out to be a blessing, not only for the women I served, but also for myself. God was faithful to His promise. As I ministered to the ladies, He was also ministering to my own heart. Through the process of sharing my personal struggles and testifying to how God was setting me free, I discovered a powerful exchange taking place. As I became more open and vulnerable, the women felt safe to do the same. They began to share with me the reasons behind their incarceration and opened up about the struggles they faced in life. This created a space where true connection and healing could begin.

Even after some of the women were released from prison, the impact of our time together remained. Several ladies reached out to let me know how much my presence and support meant to them during their time of incarceration. Hearing from them after their release affirmed that the ministry was more than just a good idea, it was a God-ordained assignment. This ministry was a source of real encouragement and transformation, both for those I served and for myself.

As I reflect on my life and the journey that brought me to this place, I realize that God was preparing me long before I ever stepped into this role. Throughout my own experiences with hurt and trauma, especially as a woman, I found myself developing a deep sensitivity to the struggles of others. I remember telling God, "Lord, I don't have to go through everything that I will have to minister to women going through." But as time went on, I learned that personal suffering shapes us in ways that allow us to truly empathize with those who are hurting.

Living with open wounds for years taught me to recognize and to be sensitive to the pain of others. When you have walked through trauma yourself, you naturally become sympathetic to those who are struggling, those who are wounded, imprisoned, or feeling unloved by others and sometimes feeling abandoned by God. This empathy is a gift that enables true ministry, as it allows us to meet people exactly where they are. God has given me not only an ear to listen but also a heart that feels deeply for the suffering of others.

The enemy's strategy is to keep God's daughters in bondage and bound by silence, shame, and fear. He wants us to remain hidden, and afraid to step into our God-given purpose. Yet, the Spirit of the Lord calls us to break free from these chains. God's message is clear: "Come out and declare your freedom." We are not meant to live in fear, but to walk boldly in the identity and purpose that God has set before us.

Through challenges I have faced and the healing I have received, I now see how God uses our stories to bring hope and encouragement to others. My journey has equipped me to minister with compassion and understanding, providing a safe space for women to find freedom and step confidently into their God-ordained destiny.

The enemy wants us to live:

- In shame – believing we are disqualified

- In grief – stuck in sorrow with no vision for joy

- In silence – afraid to speak truth or share our testimony

- In comparison – measuring our worth by others

- In rejection – believing we are unwanted

- In abandonment – feeling forgotten by God and people

But God is inviting His daughters to step out of the places where fear, shame, and secrecy have kept you bound. No longer does He desire for you to remain hidden or held back by what has happened in the past. Instead, He is calling you to leave behind the burden of shame and the weight of fear.

This call is not simply an invitation to leave something behind, but to step into something greater. God is leading His daughters into true freedom, a place where our voices are no longer silenced and our hearts are no longer burdened. He offers healing for the wounds that have caused us to shrink back, and He restores our God-given identity. In His presence, we can discover who we truly are beloved, chosen, and empowered to walk boldly in our purpose and our call. Daughters, it is time to arise; daughters it's time to come out.

- Mary Magdalene was called out of demonic torment into worship and witness.
- The woman at the well was called out of shame into Freedom.
- Hannah was called out of grief into giving birth to a prophet.
- Esther was called out of hiding into her royal purpose.
- The woman with the issue of blood was called out of isolation into restoration.

God does not just call His daughters out; He calls us up.

Declaration for the Kings Daughters to walk in Freedom:

"I will not stay in what God has called me out of. I am not bound by fear, shame, rejection or unforgiveness. I am a daughter of the King, the most High God. I am called, chosen, anointed, loved, freed, healed, delivered, and I have been made whole. I will rise up, speak up, step up, and walk in my purpose and my calling. The enemy cannot keep me in bondage to fear, pain, hurt, anger, and unforgiveness anymore, and he cannot block me, because Jesus has called me out."

CHAPTER 9

Walking in Your Freedom

Freedom, the power or right to act, speak, or think as one want. The state of not being imprisoned or enslaved.

The concept of walking in freedom in the Bible centers on the understanding that genuine freedom goes beyond simply being free from physical, internal, and external restrictions. True freedom is found within the context of a relationship with God and by following His teachings to set us free and keep us free. Freedom in Christ is not simply a single moment or breakthrough; rather, it is a lifestyle that requires intentionality and consistency every day. It is important to understand that freedom is not just about experiencing release from bondage, but it is about actively walking in that freedom and allowing it to shape our actions, thoughts, and mindset.

True freedom involves movement and transformation in how we think, believe and live. While many people may experience liberation, not everyone chooses to walk in the fullness of that freedom. Remaining in freedom means continually embracing Christ's work in our lives and refusing to return to old patterns or mentalities. It is a daily journey that calls us to live out the reality of being free, letting our renewed mindset guide our steps and decisions.

There is a story found in the Book of Exodus, the 14th chapter. In this story, Moses led the Israelites out of bondage. Their physical circumstances changed, but their mindset did not. Although they were no longer slaves in Egypt, they still carried a bondage mentality. The Israelites were set free from their oppressors, yet emotionally and mentally, they remained enslaved. This is evident in their response recorded in Exodus 14:12 (NIV) where they said, *"Didn't we say to you in Egypt, 'Leave us alone; let us serve the Egyptians'? It would have been better for us to serve the Egyptians than to die in the desert!"* Despite their newfound freedom, their thoughts and attitudes remained bound to their past. Moses successfully led them out of Egypt, but Egypt had not yet left their minds.

They were no longer under Pharaoh's rule, but the fear of Pharaoh still lingered within them. The chains that once held them were gone, yet they still longed for the familiarity and comfort of captivity. Their mentality illustrates that true freedom is not only about a change in location or circumstance, but also about transformation in how we think, believe, and live.

Nelson Mandela was a South African anti-apartheid revolutionary, political leader, and philanthropist who served as the first Black president of South Africa from 1994 to 1999. Before he served as South African's president, he was arrested in 1962 and sentenced to life imprisonment for conspiring to overthrow the government. He spent 27 years in prison. In his autobiography, "Long Walk to Freedom," Mandela wrote: "As I walked out the door toward the gate that would lead to my freedom, I knew if I didn't leave my bitterness and hatred behind, I'd still be in prison."

Mandela chose to leave bitterness and hatred behind. He chose to leave prison with a renewed mind. Transformation includes our minds being renewed, it requires an inner transformation that touches every part of our being. According to Romans 12:2, believers are instructed to *"Be transformed by the renewing of your mind."* This process is essential for walking in true freedom, as it involves a shift in how we think and perceive ourselves and our lives in the light of God's truth. Renewing your mind means replacing lies with truth. The old patterns of thinking, shaped by past experiences or bondage, must be identified and replaced with the truths found in God's Word. Only by allowing God's truth to shape our thoughts can we fully experience the transformative freedom that He offers.

When Jesus liberates someone, they are no longer bound by past limitations or false beliefs but can embrace a new reality based on God's truth. This transformation renews the mind and heart, allowing believers to fully experience lasting spiritual freedom.

The Bible is full of scriptures on freedom:

- Isaiah 61:1b – *"He has sent Me to proclaim freedom for the captives…"*

This proclamation signals not just physical release, but also emotional and spiritual freedom. The captives symbolize those held back by past fears and patterns, with God's intent being total transformation and renewing minds and breaking old cycles. Freedom here goes beyond outward change, inviting individuals to embrace a new life shaped by God's truth and to reflect His character in their actions.

- 2 Corinthians 3:17: *"Now the Lord is the Spirit, and where the Spirit of the Lord is, there is freedom."*

This verse teaches that genuine freedom comes from the Holy Spirit's presence, offering liberty beyond external conditions. The Spirit frees believers from bondage, renews their minds, and leads them to live in accordance with God's truth, enabling lasting transformation.

- Psalm 119:45: *"I will walk about in freedom, for I have sought out your precepts."*

This verse suggests that true freedom is achieved by following God's commandments. Living according to His Word allows believers to experience genuine liberation. Obedience to God's guidance frees individuals from past limitations, enabling them to live confidently and fully.

- 1 Peter 2:16: *"Live as free people, but do not use your freedom as a cover-up for evil; live as God's slaves."*

This verse teaches that freedom is not for selfishness but for living responsibly and serving others. Believers are called to use their freedom to act with love, pursue righteousness, and reflect God's character in their choices.

As we embrace the invitation to step out of fear, shame, and secrecy, and as we receive the truth of our identity as God's beloved daughters, the process of walking in freedom becomes a daily reality and one that transforms our hearts, minds, and every aspect of our lives. This journey is not marked by perfection, but by persistence: that each day, we choose to believe God's word over our past, to silence the voices that once kept us bound, and to move forward with courage into the life Christ has set before us. In these moments, freedom is not just a concept but a living experience, shaping how we see ourselves and interact with the world around us. As we continue to walk out of old mindsets and into the fullness of God's purpose, we are empowered to live boldly, speak truth, and shine as a testament to His unfailing love and a freedom that not only releases us from what held us back but propels us toward God's promise and destiny for our lives.

How to walk Step by Step in freedom

1. Be honest about your pain and hurts.
2. Be committed to ongoing healing and transformation.
3. Start each day with prayer and scripture.
4. Meditate on God's word.
5. Allow the Holy Spirit to guide your thoughts and decisions.
6. Be intentional about letting go of old fears, hurts, and unforgiveness.
7. Replace your old thoughts, and behaviors with faith-filled actions rooted in God's promises.

8. Practice self-reflection, honestly confronting areas where shame, hurts, opened wounds, secrecy and unforgiveness may linger.
9. Invite God's healing into those places.
10. Surround yourself with a community of ladies that speak life and encourage growth.
11. Be accountable for your own growth.
12. Step out in confidence, knowing that each choice to trust God moves you closer into the fullness of His purpose for you.
13. Walk boldly into all God has planned for you.

My journey has included days filled with joy and laughter, as well as moments marked by trials and tears. The loss of my brother deeply affected me, causing me to become more introverted and withdrawn. Throughout these seasons, I encountered various obstacles, but I was also blessed with experiences that felt like I was standing on the mountaintop.

In every phase of my life, God remained faithful to His promises. Even during times when I could not sense His presence, He never left my side. His steadfastness became my anchor, assuring me that I was never alone. Over time, I was transformed from being an introvert to embracing boldness through Christ. Now, I walk confidently in my calling, fully secure in my identity as a King's Daughter.

Even though challenges and adversities continue to arise, I am no longer defenseless. Where I once may have felt overwhelmed, I now recognize that I possess a weapon far greater than anything the enemy can bring against me. The Holy

Spirit stands with me as my helper and guide, providing strength and wisdom that the enemy cannot overcome. This assurance empowers me to face each battle with renewed confidence, knowing that I am never alone and that victory is possible through the help of the Holy Spirit.

So, I say to you, embrace the courage to step confidently into everything God has prepared for you. Each day, as you surrender your fears and past hurts, remember that your faith is leading you toward a greater purpose. Trust that as you let go of old habits, hurts, pain and unforgiveness and rely on God's promises, He will guide your steps. Allow yourself to walk boldly, knowing that every act of trust brings you closer to the fullness of the life God has designed for you.

May God's grace, peace and healing power be with you as you walk step by step into your freedom.

Chapter Questions and Exercises

As you work through the questions and exercises, know that your emotions may be stirred. That is a natural and important part of your healing process. Just as a wound often requires the removal of infection to fully heal, your journey may involve acknowledging, confronting, and releasing what has caused you pain. (Use a personal journal for each exercise)

Remember, as you navigate this path of healing, God is with you every step of the way.

Chapter 1: How Did I End Up Here?

Summary:

This chapter invites the reader to pause and reflect on their current life situation, how patterns, pain, or choices led to where they are today. It is about awareness without shame.

Key Themes:

- Recognizing life patterns
- Understanding roots of pain
- Awakening to self-awareness

Reflection Questions:

1. When did you first realize you were "stuck"?

   _____
   _____
   _____
   _____

2. What cycles do you see repeating in your life?

   _____
   _____
   _____
   _____

3. What emotions rise when you think about your current situation?

_____

_____

_____

_____

4. What is one truth you can hold onto as you face where you are?

_____

_____

_____

_____

Exercises:

- **Timeline Reflection:** Draw a timeline of key moments (highs/lows) that shaped your journey

- **Root Cause Worksheet:** Identify one recurring issue and list 3 possible roots.

_____

_____

_____

Prayer:
"Lord, help me see my story through Your eyes, not in shame, but with hope for transformation."

Chapter 2: Suffering in Silence

Summary:
Explores the hidden pain people carry and how silence can become a bondage. The goal is to break isolation and bring hidden wounds into the light safely.

Key Themes:

- Hidden pain & silent struggles
- The cost of isolation
- The courage to speak

Reflection Questions:

1. What areas of your life have you kept hidden?

   _____
   _____
   _____
   _____

2. Why do you find it hard to share your pain?

   _____
   _____
   _____
   _____

3. Who in your life feels "safe" enough to listen?

_____

_____

_____

_____

Exercises:

- **Letter of Release:** Write a letter (not to send) expressing what you have never said. (For this exercise, please use separate notebook paper)
- **Courage Challenge:** Share one part of your story with a trusted friend or mentor.

Prayer:

"God, give me courage to speak and healing in my voice. Let my silence be replaced by Your truth."

Chapter 3: Broken

Summary:

Addresses what it means to be broken, emotionally, spiritually, and mentally and how brokenness can become the starting point of restoration.

Key Themes:

- Brokenness is not the end
- Beauty from ashes
- Allowing God into the cracks

Reflection Questions:

1. What parts of your life feel broken?

   _____

   _____

   _____

   _____

2. How have you tried to fix your own brokenness?

   _____

   _____

   _____

   _____

3. What would it look like to invite God into your pain?

_____

_____

_____

_____

Exercises:

- **Broken Pieces Exercise:** Write each area of brokenness on small slips of paper. Pray over each one, asking God to bring healing.

- **Restoration Journal:** Write one sentence daily in a journal, beginning with "I am being restored in…"

Prayer:
"God, mend what is broken in me and turn every shattered piece into something beautiful."

Chapter 4: Living in Bondage

Summary:

Helps identify the invisible chains, fear, addiction, people-pleasing, shame that hold people captive and teaches practical steps toward spiritual and emotional freedom.

Key Themes:

- Recognizing bondage
- False comforts and strongholds
- Freedom through surrender

Reflection Questions:

1. What keeps you tied to your past?

   _____

   _____

   _____

   _____

2. What do you run to when you feel pain?

   _____

   _____

   _____

   _____

3. How has bondage disguised itself as comfort?

_____

_____

_____

_____

Exercises:

- **Chain Mapping:** Create a visual of your "chains" triggers, roots, and results.

- **Freedom Declaration:** Write: "I renounce [specific bondage], and I receive freedom through Christ."

Prayer:
"Break every chain that keeps me bound, Lord. Teach me to walk in the liberty You've already given me."

Chapter 5: What the Devil Meant for Bad...

Summary:
Reframes pain and adversity as opportunities for redemption. Highlights how God can turn what was meant for harm into a testimony of strength.

Key Themes:

- God's redemptive power
- Turning pain into purpose
- Testimony as victory

Reflection Questions:

1. What painful event has shaped your story the most?

_____

_____

_____

_____

2. How have you seen good come from a hard season?

_____

_____

_____

_____

3. What would "redemption" look like in your situation?

_____

_____

_____

_____

Exercises:

- **Victory Statement:** Write 3 sentences describing how your pain has taught you strength.

- **Testimony Prep:** Draft your 2-minute story of redemption. (use your journal for this exercise)

Prayer:

"Thank You, God, for turning my pain into power. I trust You to bring beauty from every battle."

Chapter 6: Forgiveness

Summary:
Guides readers through forgiving others and themselves to release bitterness and reclaim peace.

Key Themes:
- Forgiveness as freedom
- Releasing resentment
- Healing from within

Reflection Questions:

1. Who or what do I still hold resentment toward?

   _____

   _____

   _____

   _____

2. What has unforgiveness cost me emotionally?

   _____

   _____

   _____

   _____

3. What would forgiveness make space for in my life?

_____

_____

_____

_____

Exercises:

- **Forgiveness List:** Write names or situations you need to forgive (use your journey). Pray through each one.

- **Mirror Exercise:** Speak forgiveness over yourself aloud.

Prayer:

"Lord, teach me to forgive as You have forgiven me. Help me release the weight I have carried for too long."

Chapter 7: Finding Your Peace

Summary:

Encourages cultivating inner peace even when circumstances have not changed. Introduces daily rhythms for calm and trust.

Key Themes:

- Peace as a posture, not a place
- Guarding your heart
- Letting go of control

Reflection Questions:

1. What most often disturbs your peace?

_____

_____

_____

_____

_____

2. How can you practice stillness daily?

_____

_____

_____

_____

_____

3. What truth helps you rest in God's control?

_____

_____

_____

_____

Exercises:

- **Peace Walk:** Take a 10-minute silent walk daily, focusing on breathing and gratitude.

- **Peace Journal:** Write one thing each day that brought calm.

Prayer:

"Prince of Peace, steady my mind and calm my heart. Let Your peace rule in every storm."

Chapter 8: Declaring Your Freedom

Summary:
Teaches readers to speak truth and life replacing lies with declarations rooted in scripture and identity.

Key Themes:
- Power of spoken truth
- Identity in Christ
- Rewriting the internal narrative

Reflection Questions:

1. What lies have you believed about yourself?

   _____
   _____
   _____
   _____

2. What truth do you want to declare today?

   _____
   _____
   _____
   _____

3. How can you remind yourself of freedom daily?

_____

_____

_____

_____

Exercises:

- **Personal Declaration:** Write a one-sentence "I am free" statement for 21 days. Speak it daily.

  Truth Wall: Create a visual space for scriptures and affirmations of freedom.

Prayer:
"I declare that I am free, chosen, and whole." I walk in truth, not in fear."

Chapter 9: Walking in Your Freedom

Summary:

The culmination of the journey, learning to live free every day through consistent choices, accountability, and purpose.

Key Themes:

- Maintaining freedom
- Daily disciplines of grace
- Living with purpose and joy

Reflection Questions:

1. What does freedom look like in your daily life?

   _____

   _____

   _____

   _____

2. How will you protect your peace and progress?

   _____

   _____

   _____

   _____

3. Who can help you stay accountable in freedom?

_____

_____

_____

_____

Exercises:

- **Freedom Plan:** Write 3 daily practices that keep you spiritually strong.

- **Gratitude Habit:** End each day with one sentence of thanks for your freedom.

Prayer:
"God, help me walk in lasting freedom. Let my life be a testimony of Your power and grace."

A Declaration for Walking in Freedom:

Galatians 5:1 *"Christ has set us free! Stand, then, as free people, and do not allow yourselves to become slaves again." (GNT)*

Now write your own declaration for Walking in freedom.

_____

_____

_____

_____

_____

_____

_____

_____

_____

_____

_____

References

https://dictionary.cambridge.org/us/dictionary
https://biblehub.com/topical/a/adversary.htm
https://biblehub.com/hebrew/7651.htm
https://thedawnrehab.com/blog/childhood-trauma/
https://grammarstreet.com/2025/04/30/understanding-the-depth-of-suffering-silence
https://www.forbes.com/health/mind/anxiety-statistics
https://www.usingenglish.com/forum/threads/broken
https://www.britannica.com/biography/Nelson-Mandela

About the Author

Rev. Vivian Hart serves as a pastor in the A.M.E. Zion Church. She is the founder of "Breaking Free Bible Study and Counseling Ministry" where she ministered for five years to female inmates at Moss Justice Prison. She co-led a group of ladies for 3 years in Restoring Your Heart, a ministry under WDA. She has served on seventeen mission trips abroad. She is a graduate of Clinton College. She completed her graduate studies in Religion of Art from Lee University. Rev. Hart is also a graduate of CCI-Call Coach Institute, where she is a Certified Spirit-Led Coach. She is married to Dennis Hart, and they are the parents of three adult children, and grandparents of six grandchildren.

www.ingramcontent.com/pod-product-compliance
Lightning Source LLC
Chambersburg PA
CBHW051224120626
46547CB00013B/1495